HAUNTED OBJECTS

AROUND THE WORLD

BY MEGAN COOLEY PETERSON

CAPSTONE PRESS
a capstone imprint

Snap Books are published by
Capstone, 1710 Roe Crest Drive,
North Mankato, Minnesota 56003.
www.mycapstone.com

For information regarding permission, write to Capstone, 1710 Roe Crest Drive, North Mankato, Minnesota 56003.

Library of Congress Cataloging-in-Publication Data
Library of Congress Cataloging-in-Publication data is available on the Library of Congress website.
ISBN 978-1-5157-3859-6 (hardcover)
ISBN 978-1-5157-3867-1 (eBook PDF)

Editorial Credits
Mari Bolte, editor; Kristi Carlson, designer; Wanda Winch, media researcher; Gene Bentdahl, production specialist

Photo Credits
Alamy: Design Pics, Inc, 6; Courtesy of Abigaile Moon, 22, 23; Courtesy of James Angus, 7, 8, 9; Courtesy of the Thirsk Museum, 28; iStockphoto: James Carroll, 24; Jason Butler, 12, 15; Newscom: Everett Collection, 16; Shutterstock: Alina G, 29, A-R-T, calligraphic design, Checubus, 10, Fantom666, grunge background, HiSunnySky, floral background, ilolab, brick wall design, jakkapan, retro frame design, Jakub Krechowicz, 5, janniwet, antique frame, Jaroslav Moravcik, 17, Joe Parchatree, 21, kzww, wood wall, Leremy, ornate sign design, LilGraphie, photo corners design, LovArt, globe design, Marco Barone, cover (bottom), Olga Labusova, 27, PeterPhoto123, oval frame, Pictures_for_You, cover (middle), Rachelle Burnside, cover (top left), rayjunk, vintage frame, Shelly Still, cover (top right), spaxiax, stone wall background, Suzanne Tucker, 11, Vera Petruk, 13, VitalyRomanovich, 19; Thinkstock: pawopa3336, 26; TheAnguishedMan.com, 18; Wikimedia: Pubdog, 20

Printed in China.
092016   007892

TABLE OF CONTENTS

HANDLE WITH CARE

It's late at night as you and your friend sneak up into the attic. Trunks and boxes hold old clothing and books. Your friend accidentally backs into a mirror, and the yellowed sheet covering it falls to the floor. A face flashes in the shiny glass. It was probably just your friend's face—or was it? You turn on a radio, and it crackles to life. Suddenly the sound of laughter erupts from the speakers. Could the mirror and radio be haunted? Or is your imagination getting the better of you.

For thousands of years, people have wondered if ghosts exist. Can the spirits of the dead haunt the living? Some people think ghosts can even haunt objects. Perhaps the object was important to the ghost while he or she was alive.

Even today no one knows for sure if ghosts exist. But the people in this book claim they've encountered actual haunted objects. Decide for yourself if these stories are real or not.

Moving eyes, real, humanlike features, and many potential owners—no wonder dolls are commonly haunted objects!

Be Spooked ... In Person!

There are museums full of haunted objects throughout the world. For a small fee, you can see the spooky things collectors have found over the years.

The Traveling Museum of the Paranormal & Occult claims to be the world's only mobile museum. Every year it travels to conventions, haunted locations, and private events to scare and delight audiences across America.

ROBERT THE DOLL

Attics and basements are often filled with old objects.
Could some of those objects be haunted?

Most dolls are made of fabric, stuffing, and button eyes. Robert the doll may have been made with a little something extra.

In 1904, four-year-old Robert Eugene Otto received a special doll. The doll stood 40 inches (102 centimeters) tall and wore a sailor's outfit. Legend says the doll was made to look like Robert, who named the doll after himself. He started calling himself Gene.

Young Gene took Robert everywhere he went. When Gene got in trouble, he blamed Robert. Gene's parents often heard their son talking to Robert at night. The doll would reply in a strange voice. His parents assumed Gene used a different voice for Robert.

Robert and his stuffed dog were donated to the Key West Art & Historical Society's Fort East Martello Museum in 1994.

FACT

Legend says the doll's hair was made from human hair. Actually Robert's hair is made of a yarnlike material.

When Gene grew up and got married, he and his bride moved into his childhood home in Florida. The couple had a permanent roommate—Robert the doll. Gene even built Robert a special room in the attic. He filled the room with furniture just for Robert.

Gene, a talented artist, often painted in the attic with Robert. Children walking by the house said they saw Robert moving in the window. Was it really Robert? Or could they have been seeing Gene?

Today Gene's home is known as the Artist House.
It has been a hotel since 1978.

NEW OWNERS

Gene died in 1974. His wife moved out of the house and left Robert behind. When Myrtle Reuter bought Gene's house, she became Robert's new owner. She claimed the doll was haunted and moved on its own. A plumber working alone in the attic heard giggling. When he turned around, Robert had moved across the room. One reporter claimed that Robert's face changed expression during a conversation. "The doll was listening to us," he said.

Myrtle donated Robert to a museum before she died in the mid-1990s. The strange events didn't stop. Cameras and other electronic devices failed to work when in the doll's presence. Today Robert lives in a glass box at the museum. Guests sometimes claim that they see Robert moving. Are you brave enough to visit him?

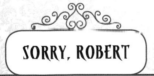

SORRY, ROBERT

Notes and cards surround Robert's display case at the Fort East Martello Museum. Some are friendly messages, but many are letters of apology. Visitors who don't ask the doll's permission before snapping photos run into bad luck. One woman claims Robert made her cat bite her. After mocking Robert, another visitor missed his flight home. Robert even has his own e-mail address so fans can write to him.

GAMING WITH GHOSTS

Estate sales, storage spaces, and thrift stores are all places to find unusual—and sometimes haunted—objects.

Can video gaming systems communicate with the dead? In 2005 a gamer bought a **vintage** Nintendo Entertainment System (NES) from a thrift store in Brooklyn, New York. The store owner said a man brought it in. It belonged to his son who died years ago.

The gamer brought the NES home and switched it on. Within minutes, he heard human voices coming from the machine. When he paused the game, the voices stopped.

> **vintage:** from the past

The strange occurrences continued. Sometimes the game would pause by itself. The gamer bought new controls. But the game continued to act on its own. The gamer sold the NES on eBay later that year. Its haunted status is still discussed today.

Did the machine have a glitch? Was its owner simply looking for fame? Or was someone from beyond the grave trying to make contact? You decide.

GHOSTS FOR SALE

The popular website eBay sells everything from clothing to cars. It even sells haunted items. Fans of the paranormal can buy allegedly haunted dolls, jewelry, and even teapots on the site. Buyer beware!

AMAZING ANNABELLE

Annabelle seemed to move from room to room on her own.

In 1970 a nursing student named Donna unwrapped a birthday gift from her mother. It was a Raggedy Ann doll purchased from a craft store.

Donna and her roommate noticed strange things about the doll. They found pieces of parchment paper with the words "Help us" written on it. Neither roommate wrote the notes. Even stranger—they didn't keep parchment paper in the apartment.

THE SÉANCE

One night Donna arrived home to her apartment. She found red drops on the doll's hands and chest. She hadn't spilled anything on the doll. Fearing it was blood, Donna contacted a **medium**. Together they held a **séance**. The medium said a girl's spirit was attached to the doll. The girl's name was Annabelle Higgins. She died long before Donna's apartment building had been built.

Special objects, such as tarot cards, rune stones, and séance boards, can be used to conduct a séance.

According to the medium, Annabelle was lonely. She wanted to be friends with Donna and her roommate. Donna felt bad for Annabelle and said the ghost could stay.

FACT

The story of Annabelle was made into a 2014 movie. However, in the movie, she is a much more sinister-looking porcelain doll.

medium: a person who claims to make contact with ghosts

séance: a meeting at which people attempt to make contact with the dead

LOU'S STORY

Annabelle gave Donna's friend Lou the creeps. While asleep at the apartment, he claimed Annabelle crawled up his legs. Lou couldn't move as the doll crept closer to his face. He gasped as Annabelle strangled him. His vision went black.

Lou awoke the next morning. Had it all been a bad dream? Then he heard movement in Donna's bedroom. Donna wasn't home. Afraid someone had broken in, Lou rushed into her room. It was empty—except for Annabelle. As he approached the doll, he sensed someone behind him. Lou spun around, but no one was there.

Without warning, pain shot through Lou's chest. Blood seeped through his shirt. When he opened his shirt, he saw seven claw marks on his chest.

Donna became convinced Annabelle was not a kind ghost. She contacted the priest at her church. Her priest then called **paranormal investigators** Ed and Lorraine Warren. The Warrens concluded that a **demon** had possessed the doll. It only pretended to be the ghost of a little girl. The demon's ultimate goal was human possession. The Warrens found a priest to perform an **exorcism**.

---

paranormal investigator: someone who studies events that science can't explain

demon: an evil, inhuman spirit

exorcism: the act of freeing a person or place from an evil spirit

---

GONE BUT NOT FORGOTTEN

The Warrens took Annabelle home after the exorcism. Ed put the doll in the backseat. During the drive, the car stalled many times. The brakes failed. Finally Ed sprinkled Annabelle with holy water.

The doll caused no further trouble—until they arrived home. Annabelle floated into the air. The doll moved from room to room. A man who taunted Annabelle soon died in a motorcycle accident.

Ed and Lorraine decided to lock up the doll. They built a special glass case. Annabelle resides there to this day.

Today Annabelle is locked in a case marked, "Warning: Positively Do Not Open."

THE WARRENS

Ed and Lorraine Warren have consulted on many paranormal cases. In 1952 they founded the New England Society for Psychic Research. The Warrens claim to have investigated more than 10,000 cases.

The Amityville haunting is the Warren's most famous case. The Lutz family claimed a demonic spirit haunted their home. Ed and Lorraine visited the house 20 days after the family fled. Many skeptics doubt the Amityville case. But the Warrens said it was not a hoax.

TUT'S TOMB

The discovery of Tut's tomb—and the supposed curse that went along with it—fascinated people around the world.

Kｉng Tut ruled near the end of Egypt's 18th dynasty. Unfortunately the boy king did not have a long rule. When he died, his tomb was filled with items the **pharaoh** needed for the afterlife. There were more than 5,000 treasures, including a solid-gold coffin to hold his mummy.

In 1922 his tomb was found in the Valley of the Kings by archaeologist Howard Carter. Unlike many previously-discovered sites, Tut's tomb remained untouched by thieves and grave robbers. It was a great discovery.

> **pharaoh:** a king of ancient Egypt

Yet, eight of the people involved with unearthing his tomb passed away within 12 years. Lord Carnarvon, the man who funded the dig, died from blood poisoning after being bitten by a mosquito. A friend of Howard Carter was given a mummified hand as a gift. The man's house burned down—twice. Were the objects in Tut's tomb cursed? Or was it just bad luck?

King Tut's mummy rested inside a solid-gold coffin.

FACT

Rumors say Howard Carter was the one who invented the story of the mummy's curse. He wanted to keep news reporters and thieves away. He also managed to avoid the curse, living until 1939.

THE ANGUISHED MAN

Art can inspire. It can make people forget their troubles. But some of it can truly terrify. Be careful the next time you admire a work of art.

To this day, nobody knows who really painted the Anguished Man.

Sean Robinson's grandmother kept a strange painting in her attic. The canvas showed a man's face twisted in agony. The man had black holes for eyes. He seemed to be screaming. Sean's grandmother said the painting's artist had mixed his own blood with the paint. Shortly after completing the painting, the artist supposedly died. Did he take his own life—or was there a scarier explanation?

Years later, Sean inherited the painting. Soon after he brought it home, strange things happened. He heard scraping sounds in the basement, where the painting was kept. Fog would suddenly appear at the top of the stairs and then vanish. Sean saw the figure of a man. His wife felt a hand touch her hair. People who viewed the painting got nosebleeds. Some felt extreme nausea.

In 2010 Sean decided to film the painting. He left it in a spare bedroom, turned on a camera, and went to sleep. The bedroom door shut on its own. The camera also recorded a loud banging sound. When Sean inspected the room, nothing had fallen. Today Sean keeps the painting locked away.

Sobbing and crying was heard from inside Sean's house. Sometimes it sounded like it was coming from the Robinsons' bedroom.

FACT

You can see Sean Robinson's video recordings of the painting on YouTube.

THE BAKER MANSION GOWN

**Construction on the Baker Mansion started in 1845.
It was completed in 1849.**

A beautiful wedding gown can become a work of art. For Anna Baker, it may have become an obsession—from beyond the grave.

Anna Baker lived at the Baker mansion in Altoona, Pennsylvania. She fell in love with a poor man and wanted to get married. But Anna's father, a wealthy businessman, forbade it. Anna never married. Some say she died of a broken heart in 1914.

After Anna's death the Baker mansion was turned into a museum. The museum dedicated a room to another local wealthy family, the Bells. The room displayed Elizabeth Bell's wedding dress in a glass case.

Museum staff said the dress danced by itself—especially during full moons. Sometimes the dress shook so violently staff members worried the case might break. Stories say Anna's ghost hated the dress because she never got to wear it.

Legend says that Anna remained angry at her father for the rest of her life. Could that rage exist from beyond the grave?

FACT

According to some sources, the wedding dress had originally belonged to Anna Baker. Then Elizabeth Bell bought it for her own ceremony—which may have upset Anna's ghost even more.

THE MIRROR AT MYRTLES PLANTATION

Myrtles Plantation was built in 1796 in Louisiana.

Myrtles Plantation is said to be the most haunted house in the United States. Several people were allegedly murdered in the house. As the tale goes, a slave girl named Chloe was caught eavesdropping. As punishment, the plantation owner cut off her ear. To get revenge, Chloe poisoned his wife and children.

Years later, William Winter and his family owned the home. One day, while leaving his house, he was shot on the front porch by an unknown man. He managed to make his way back into the house and partially up the stairway before dying. Guests today say they can hear his ghost struggling up the stairs to his final place of death.

Many visitors have reported ghostly activity around the plantation. The spirits may be drawn to the plantation by a gold-framed mirror that hangs on the first floor of the mansion. Some believe the spirits of those who died there live inside the mirror. Handprints suddenly appear on the glass. Drip marks ooze down its shiny surface. Staff members have tried to clean the mirror, but the strange spots return. Some visitors have reported seeing people wearing old-fashioned clothing in the mirror's reflection—but not inside the house itself.

The spirits of the plantation owner's murdered family are said to be trapped in the mirror.

MAGIC MIRROR

Objects that reflect images—such as crystal balls, mirrors, and even flat pans of water—have been used for paranormal activities for centuries. Scrying mirrors were used for fortune telling. By staring into the mirror, the fortune teller tried to "see" the future.

A CURSED CABINET

In 2001 Kevin Mannis bought an antique wooden cabinet at a yard sale. He was told the cabinet had belonged to a 103-year-old woman who recently died. Before her death, she claimed the cabinet was haunted and warned her family never to open it. Kevin didn't listen. Inside the box he found locks of hair, pennies, and a dried rosebud.

The haunted cabinet is more famously known as the
Dybbuk (or Dibbuk) Box.

GET OUT!

A dybbuk is a supernatural creature from Jewish folktales. It is an evil wandering spirit that takes over a person's body. Only an exorcism can get the dybbuk to leave.

Kevin brought the cabinet to his furniture store. He placed it in the basement where he planned to clean it. One day, he received a frantic phone call from his employee. All the light bulbs in the basement had exploded. The employee heard screaming—but she was the only one in the store. She quit and never returned.

A few weeks later, Kevin's mother came to his store. It was her birthday, and Kevin gave her the cabinet. He left the room to make a phone call. Suddenly an employee burst into his office—something was wrong with Kevin's mother. They found her frozen next to the cabinet, unable to speak. She had suffered a **stroke**.

The cabinet changed hands several times. Kevin's sister said the doors opened on their own. She returned it. A couple who bought the cabinet left it outside the store. A note attached to the cabinet said, "This has a bad darkness."

Kevin soon began having terrible nightmares. Other members of his family had the same nightmares. Kevin wondered if the cabinet really *was* haunted. Afraid to destroy it, he sold the cabinet on eBay.

FACT

The Dybbuk Box's current owner says the cabinet reversed his aging. He keeps it locked away.

stroke: a medical condition that occurs when a blocked blood vessel stops oxygen from reaching the brain

A DEAD MAN'S CHAIR

Busby's chair—also known as Busby's Stoop Chair of Death and the Dead Man's Chair—is far from the only haunted piece of furniture to exist.

In 1702 **counterfeiter** Thomas Busby went to his favorite pub in Yorkshire, England. When he arrived, his father-in-law was already sitting in Thomas' usual chair. The two had been partners, but their relationship had recently turned sour. His father-in-law no longer approved of Thomas' marriage to his daughter. He told Thomas he was taking her away and left the pub.

counterfeiter: someone who makes fake things that look real

Later that night, Thomas crept into his father-in-law's house and killed him. Thomas was convicted and hanged. Moments before his death, Thomas spit a warning at the crowd. He said anyone who sat in his chair at the pub would meet an untimely death.

Several decades passed and nothing happened. Then one day a chimney sweep stopped into the pub for lunch. There was only one seat available—Thomas Busby's favorite chair. He ignored the legend and sat down. An hour later, the chimney sweep fell off a roof and died.

For many years, hanging was the most severe punishment for criminals.

THE CURSE OR JUST BAD LUCK?

Soldiers frequented the pub during World War II (1939–1945). They often dared each other to sit in Thomas Busby's chair. According to legend, those who sat in it never returned from the war.

In 1967 a pair of pilots thought it would be fun to sit in Thomas' chair. Soon after leaving the pub, the pilots allegedly lost control of their car. It crashed into a tree and burst into flames. Both men died.

Today Busby's stoop chair hangs on the wall of the Cottage Kitchen display at the Thirsk Museum.

A DANGEROUS CHAIR

The chair was soon moved into the pub's basement. But that didn't stop a bricklayer from taking a seat. Legend has it that he died in an accident less than an hour later. Was it a coincidence? Or was Thomas Busby's chair really haunted?

In 1978 the pub owner decided it was too dangerous to keep the chair. He donated it to a museum in Thirsk, England. Museum staff members hung the chair on the wall so no one would accidentally sit in it.

Unlike a haunted house, hotel, or area, haunted objects are small. They can easily be lost or be passed from person to person. You might own a haunted object and not even know it—that is, until it's too late.

FACT OR FICTION?

No one knows for certain if haunted objects exist. Movies, TV, books, and the internet are filled with paranormal stories. Skeptics say these stories trick people into believing in ghosts and haunted objects. But witnesses say their experiences really happened. If you see an allegedly haunted object, think twice before touching it.

GLOSSARY

counterfeit (KAUN-tuhr-fit)—something fake that looks like the real thing, such as counterfeit money

demon (DE-muhn)—an evil, inhuman spirit

exorcism (EK-suhr-siz-uhm)—the act of freeing a person or place from an evil spirit

ghost (GOHST)—a spirit of a dead person believed to haunt people or places

hoax (HOHKS)—a trick to make people believe something that is not true

legend (LEJ-uhnd)—a story handed down from earlier times that could seem believable

medium (MEE-dee-um)—a person who claims to make contact with ghosts

paranormal investigator (pa-ruh-NOR-muhl in-VESS-tuhgate-ur)—someone who studies events that science can't explain

pharaoh (FAIR-oh)—a king of ancient Egypt

séance (SAY-ahnss)—a meeting at which people attempt to make contact with the dead

skeptic (SKEP-tik)—someone who doubts or questions beliefs

spirit (SPIHR-it)—the invisible part of a person that contains thoughts and feelings; some people believe the spirit leaves the body after death

stroke (STROHK)—a medical condition that occurs when a blocked blood vessel stops oxygen from reaching the brain

vintage (VIN-tij)—from the past

READ MORE

Bolte, Mari. *Encountering Ghosts: Eyewitness Accounts*. North Mankato, Minn.: Capstone Press, 2015.

Ramsey, Grace. *Haunted Objects*. Vero Beach, Fla.: Rourke Pub. Group, 2016.

Seeley, M.H. *Freaky Stories about the Paranormal*. Freaky True Science. New York: Gareth Stevens Publishing, 2016.

INTERNET SITES

FactHound offers a safe, fun way to find Internet sites related to this book. All of the sites on FactHound have been researched by our staff.

Here's all you do:
Visit *www.facthound.com*
Type in this code: 9781515738596

Check out projects, games and lots more at
www.capstonekids.com

INDEX

READ ALL THE IT'S HAUNTED TITLES!
Titles in This Set

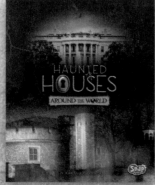